HOW TO MEASURE

Time with a Calendar

Darice Bailer

LIGHTBOX
openlightbox.com

LIGHTBOX

Go to
www.openlightbox.com
and enter this book's
unique code.

ACCESS CODE

LBS43978

Lightbox is an all-inclusive digital solution for the teaching and learning of curriculum topics in an original, groundbreaking way. Lightbox is based on National Curriculum Standards.

STANDARD FEATURES OF LIGHTBOX

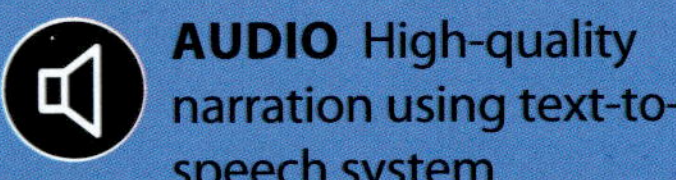
AUDIO High-quality narration using text-to-speech system

ACTIVITIES Printable PDFs that can be emailed and graded

SLIDESHOWS Pictorial overviews of key concepts

VIDEOS Embedded high-definition video clips

WEBLINKS Curated links to external, child-safe resources

TRANSPARENCIES Step-by-step layering of maps, diagrams, charts, and timelines

INTERACTIVE MAPS Interactive maps and aerial satellite imagery

QUIZZES Ten multiple choice questions that are automatically graded and emailed for teacher assessment

KEY WORDS Matching key concepts to their definitions

Contents

Lightbox Access Code 2

What Is a Calendar? 4

Calendar Timeline................. 7

How Does a Calendar Work? 8

A Monthly Plan 12

From Words to Numbers 16

Record-Setting Calendars 20

Quiz 22

Key Words / Index 23

www.openlightbox.com ... 24

July

Sunday	Monday	Tuesday	Wednesday	Thursday	Friday	Saturday
	1	2	3	4	5	6
7	8	9	10	11	12	13
14	15	16	17	18	19	20
21	22	23	24	25	26	27
28	29	30	31			

What Is a Calendar?

How many **days** until your friend's sleepover? How many **weeks** until your birthday party? How many **months** until winter?

The idea of birthday cakes came from Germany. The first birthday cakes were only for children.

The coldest U.S. winter on record was from 1978 to 1979. Many places were 16° Fahrenheit (9° Celsius) colder than normal.

We can use a **calendar** to measure time. A calendar keeps track of the days, weeks, and months of the **year**.

The world record for the **oldest person** is **122 years old**.

Every day, almost **20 million** people celebrate their **birthday**.

The world's **oldest** known calendar is from **10,000 years** ago.

A calendar helps you know when school starts. You see when holidays will happen. You can count the weeks until your birthday. Or count the days until your family trip. Let's measure time with a calendar!

To do the activities in this book, you will need:

- 12 index cards or small pieces of paper
- 2 dice
- watch with a hand that counts seconds
- scissors
- marker

Calendar Timeline

2400 BC The Sumerians use a **lunar** calendar. The calendar has 12 months. Each month has 29 or 30 days.

104 BC A Chinese calendar is used throughout the country. Every year is named after a different animal. The animals are Rat, Ox, Tiger, Rabbit, Dragon, Snake, Horse, Goat, Monkey, Rooster, Dog, and Pig.

45 BC The Julian calendar is invented in Rome. It is named after Julius Caesar. The calendar is used across Europe.

1582 AD The Gregorian calendar is made and spreads across the world. It makes the Julian calendar more accurate. This is the calendar most people use today.

1870 The United States adds federal holidays to calendars. Government workers are given four paid days off. Six more are later added.

1990s Calendars go digital. Personal digital assistants (PDAs) become popular. These small computers let people keep their calendar in the palm of their hand.

Sunday

Monday

Tuesday

Wednesday

Thursday

Friday

Saturday

How Does a Calendar Work?

Days of the Week
Sunday
Monday
Tuesday
Wednesday
Thursday
Friday
Saturday

There are seven days in a week. Can you name them? What is your favorite day of the week?

Add up all the weeks. There are 52 each year.

And there are 12 months for you to count. February is the shortest month. It has 28 or 29 days. The other months have 30 or 31 days.

Months of the Year

January	February	March	April	May	June

Activity

What's Missing?

Two months are missing here. Which are they?

July	August	September	October	November	December

Use a poem to remember how many days are in each month.

Thirty days in September,
April, June, and November.
February has 28 days, but to be clear
It leaps to 29 every four years!
Then there are 7 months with 31 days that fly
March, May, August, and July
And 31 days to also remember
In January, October, and December!

January is the first month of the year. December is the twelfth and last. Then a whole new year begins on January 1!

Many people stay up late on December 31. The New Year officially begins at midnight, or 12:00 a.m.

Activity

The Months of the Year

Instructions:

1. Take 12 index cards. Small pieces of paper work, too. Write the name of one month on each card. Stack them up in a pile.

2. Find or borrow a watch with a second hand. And find a friend.

3. Mix up all the index cards.

4. Work together to put the months in order. Use the watch to time yourselves. Now try to beat your team time!

A Monthly Plan

Zara and Carter are getting ready for summer. They're making a calendar for July. They want to plan for Zara's swim class. Carter's grandma is coming to visit, too.

More than half of U.S. students do after-school activities, including sports. Calendars help them stay organized.

Carter drew all the rows and **columns** with a ruler. Then Zara wrote the month and the days of the week at the top.

July

Sunday	Monday	Tuesday	Wednesday	Thursday	Friday	Saturday

In North America, most calendars start weeks with Sunday. In Europe, they usually start with Monday.

Zara and Carter check their calendar. They can see on which day of the week each **date** falls. They can keep track of their summer fun.

People are often busier on Tuesdays than other days of the week.

Activity

Can you help Zara and Carter figure a few things out this summer?

Instructions:

1. Carter and Zara are watching the fireworks on July 4. What day of the week is it?
2. Carter's grandma is coming to visit on the Monday after July 4. What date does her visit begin?
3. Carter's grandma is leaving on July 20. What day of the week is that?
4. Zara has a swim meet every Monday in July. How many times will she race with the team this summer?
5. Can Carter's grandma go to any of Zara's swim meets? Which ones can she see?
6. Carter's birthday is five days before his grandma leaves. When is his birthday?

July

Sunday	Monday	Tuesday	Wednesday	Thursday	Friday	Saturday
	1	2	3	4	5	6
7	8	9	10	11	12	13
14	15	16	17	18	19	20
21	22	23	24	25	26	27
28	29	30	31			

From Words to Numbers

Carter wonders why some years have 365 days but a **leap year** has 366. Zara knows the answer!

A person born on a leap day is sometimes called a leapling or a leaper.

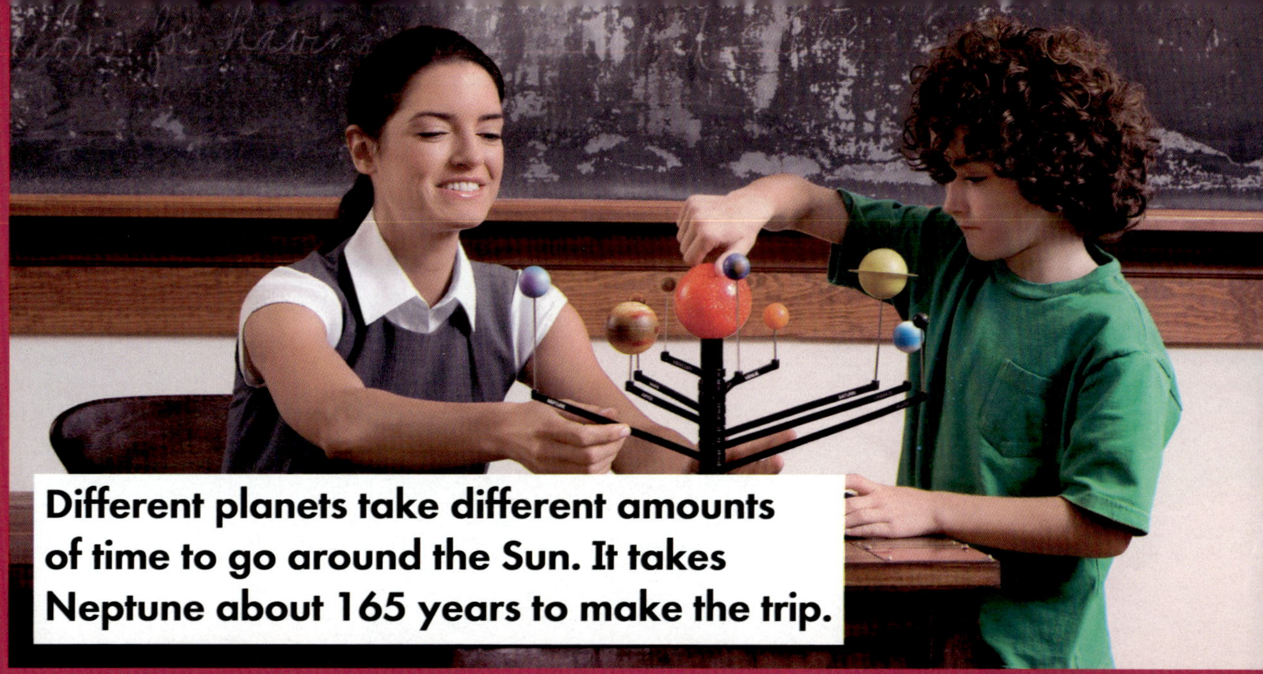

Different planets take different amounts of time to go around the Sun. It takes Neptune about 165 years to make the trip.

It takes Earth one year, or 365 days, 5 hours, and a little over 48 minutes, to go around the Sun. But a calendar year is only 365 days long. So every year on the calendar is a little shorter than an actual year. The fourth year has one day added to make up for that.

The **odds** of being born on **February 29** are **1** in **1,461**.

FEB
29

In **Ireland**, it is tradition for women to ask men to **marry** them on February 29.

In the United States, new **presidents** are **elected** during leap years.

More people are born in September than any other month.

Zara wants to write down her birthday using all numbers. She learned how to do it in school. The teacher wrote the date on the board each day. Zara knows that March is the third month. She writes her birthday two ways: March 31, 2008, and 3/31/2008.

Zara shows Carter how to write his birthday with numbers, too. Carter's birthday is July 15, 2006. Carter writes 7/15/2006. He can shorten it to 7/15/06. Or he can put the year first, 2006/7/15.

Activity

Monthly Roll

Take turns rolling a pair of dice with a friend. Then call out the name of the month that goes with that number. For example, if you roll a two, shout, "February!" February is the second month of the year.

Now play the game a different way. Roll one die. Call out the month. It will be one of the first six months of the year. Then roll the second die. Count forward that many months. For example, suppose you roll a one with the first die. You would call out, "January!" Then you roll a five. What month comes five months after January?

There are 36 different outcomes when rolling two dice. When three dice are rolled, there are 216.

Record-Setting Calendars

There are many record-setting calendars in the United States. Some of these are the most popular or oldest calendars in the nation, or even in the world.

Pacific Ocean

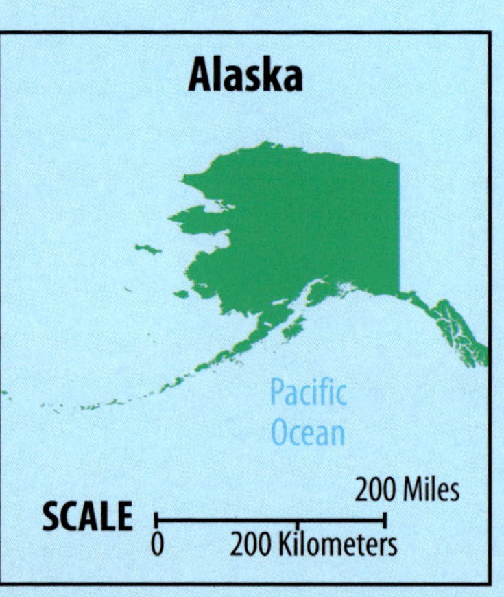

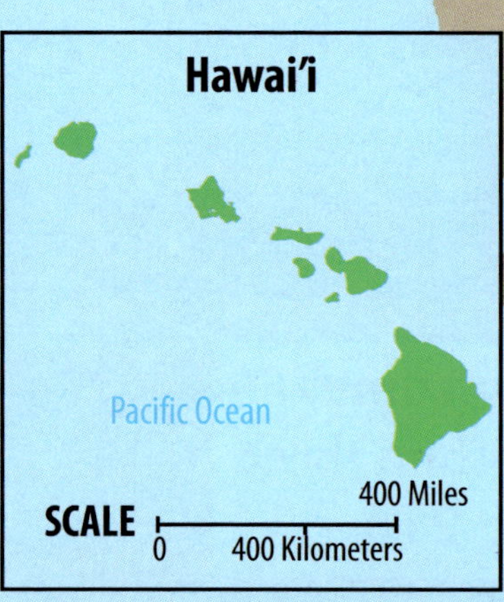

Big Horn Medicine Wheel
Lovell, Wyoming
Plains Indians built the Big Horn Medicine Wheel between 300 and 800 years ago. The wheel, made of stones, uses the stars to keep track of time. It is one of the oldest calendars found in the United States.

The Old Farmer's Almanac

Dublin, New Hampshire

The Old Farmer's **Almanac** was started in 1792 to help farmers time their crops. It is still published today, with headquarters in Dublin, New Hampshire. This makes it the longest-running calendar in the United States. More than 3 million copies are sold each year.

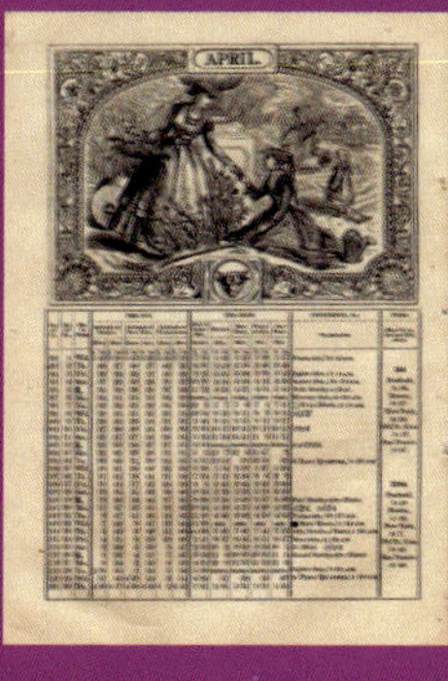

North Dakota
Minnesota
South Dakota
Wisconsin
Michigan
Nebraska
Iowa
Kansas
Missouri
Illinois
Indiana
Ohio
Kentucky
West Virginia
Virginia
Tennessee
North Carolina
Oklahoma
Pennsylvania
New York
Maine
Vermont
New Hampshire
Massachusetts
Rhode Island
Connecticut
New Jersey
Delaware
Maryland
Atlantic Ocean

Workman Publishing Company

New York City, New York

The Workman Publishing Company is one of the biggest calendar companies in the United States. They invented Page-A-Day desk calendars in 1979. The small calendars have one page for each day. More than 200 million have been sold.

LEGEND

- United States
- Other Countries
- City
- Water

N S E W

SCALE 0 250 Miles 250 Kilometers

1 What does a calendar keep track of?

2 What is the calendar people use today called?

3 When were federal holidays added to U.S. calendars?

4 How many weeks are there each year?

5 Which is the shortest month?

6 On what day does a new year begin?

7 In North America, most calendars start with which day?

8 On which day do people tend to be most busy?

9 How many days does a leap year have?

10 How can you write July 15, 2006, using only numbers?

Answers: 1. Days, weeks, and months **2.** The Gregorian calendar **3.** 1870 **4.** 52 **5.** February **6.** January 1 **7.** Sunday **8.** Tuesday **9.** 366 **10.** 7/15/2006, 7/15/06, or 2006/7/15

Key Words

almanac: an annual calendar with information on the weather, moon cycles, tides, and other topics

calendar: a chart to help you keep track of the days, weeks, and months of the year

columns: lines of numbers or words going up and down

date: a specific day

days: periods of 24 hours from midnight to midnight

leap year: the year every four years when an extra day is added to February for a total of 366 days

lunar: having to do with the moon and its cycles

months: the 12 unequal periods that make up the year

weeks: periods of seven days

year: a measure of time with 12 months and four seasons

Index

Big Horn Medicine Wheel 20
birthdays 4, 5, 6, 15, 18

Chinese calendar 7
columns 13

dates 14, 15, 18
days 4, 5, 6, 7, 8, 10, 13, 14, 15, 16, 17, 18, 21, 22
days in each month 10

Earth 17

Gregorian calendar 7, 22

holidays 6, 7, 22

Julian calendar 7

leap years 16, 17, 22
lunar calendar 7

months 4, 5, 7, 8, 9, 10, 11, 13, 18, 19, 22

The Old Farmer's Almanac 21

rows 13

Sun 17

visit 12, 15

weeks 4, 5, 6, 8, 13, 14, 15, 22
Workman Publishing Company 21

years 5, 7, 8, 10, 16, 17, 18, 19, 20, 21, 22

SUPPLEMENTARY RESOURCES

Click on the plus icon found in the bottom left corner of each spread to open additional teacher resources.

- Download and print the book's quizzes and activities
- Access curriculum correlations
- Explore additional web applications that enhance the Lightbox experience

LIGHTBOX DIGITAL TITLES
Packed full of integrated media

VIDEOS

INTERACTIVE MAPS

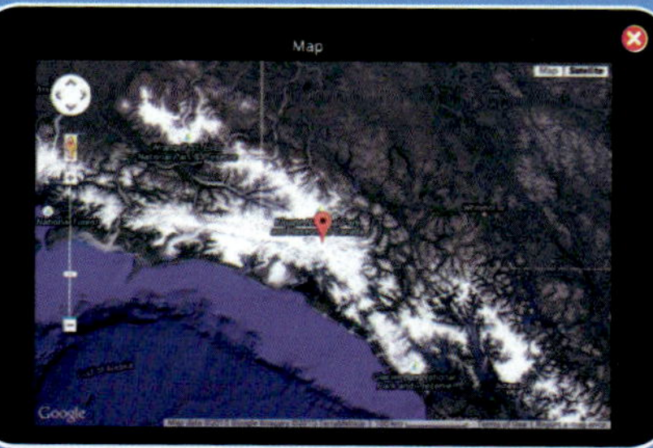

WEBLINKS

SLIDESHOWS

QUIZZES

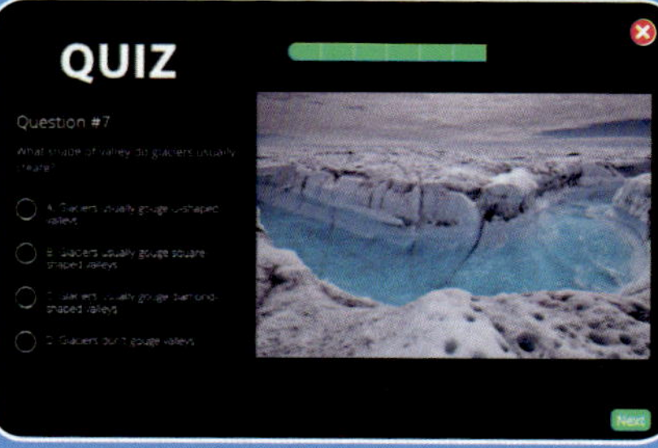

OPTIMIZED FOR

- ✓ TABLETS
- ✓ WHITEBOARDS
- ✓ COMPUTERS
- ✓ AND MUCH MORE!

Published by Smartbook Media Inc. 350 5th Avenue, 59th Floor New York, NY 10118
Website: www.openlightbox.com

012018
120517

Library of Congress Control Number: 2017960151

ISBN 978-1-5105-3632-6 (hardcover)
ISBN 978-1-5105-3633-3 (multi-user eBook)

Printed in the Brainerd, Minnesota, United States
1 2 3 4 5 6 7 8 9 0 22 21 20 19 18

First published by Cherry Lake in 2014.

Project Coordinator: John Willis
Designer: Ana María Vidal

Every reasonable effort has been made to trace ownership and to obtain permission to reprint copyright material. The publisher would be pleased to have any errors or omissions brought to its attention so that they may be corrected in subsequent printings.

The publisher acknowledges Alamy, Getty Images, and iStock as the primary image suppliers for this title.